TOP 100 CRYPTOCURRENCIES

Mastering Cryptocurrencies

Leo Nordbo

Northern Light Publishing

CONTENTS

INTRODUCTION

I am a computer science student and I felt like there was a void in crypto currency literature that needed to be filled out with a book that goes through the top 100 crypto currencies. I hope that this book will fill out that void.

Addresses for tips

Cardano (ADA):
DdzFFzCqrhssXe9GtiYjbsLP5KhWJ4SZ3BsHvSTKTCHqnCe-SoUK5cwZEgzSyFqfAHoUC3sPYRAinY8rAJYcxnDLao8w-coKYmE5jKGvNx

Ethereum(ETH):
0x76b59e6851f9a1eCC732afF9cA584b21Cde84bb1

Bitcoin (XBT):
3HruA3bKy5U7hAJ4NxCaKA2XxUBruHNgBr

ABOUT BITCOIN

What Is Bitcoin?

Bitcoin is a completely decentralized digital cryptocurrency. Unlike US dollars that you can hold in your hand (or in your bank account), there is no central authority or centralized payment system controlling Bitcoin. Instead, Bitcoin operates in a peer-to-peer network that allows anyone in the world to send and receive Bitcoin without any middleman (like a bank, central bank or payment processor).

Bitcoin was the very first cryptocurrency ever created. On Oct. 31, 2008 a person (or group of people) under the pseudonym "Satoshi Nakamoto" published the now-world famous Bitcoin whitepaper

The first line reads: "A purely peer-to-peer version of electronic cash, which would allow online payments to be sent directly from one party to another without going through a financial institution."

The Bitcoin network then launched on Jan. 3, 2009, marking the start of the cryptocurrency revolution.

How Does Bitcoin Work?

Bitcoin is a purely decentralized digital currency, which makes it unlike any other asset that came before it.

Before the digital age, everyone transacted in physical forms of currencies, from livestock and salt, to silver and gold, and finally to banknotes. Only in recent times was money "digitized" — allowing bank accounts to exist online, as well as creating the many online payment processing platforms, such as PayPal and Square, that you often use today without thinking about it.

However, all of these "digital transactions" require a centralized system to operate. Your bank, or financial services like PayPal, needs to ensure that all of their users' accounts are constantly updated and tallied correctly. These systems represent the centralized form of digital money.

Bitcoin revolutionized digital money by decentralizing this accounting process. Instead of a central figure that is responsible for making sure that their users' transactions were always adding up, Bitcoin works by sharing the account balances and transactions of every user across the globe in a pseudonymous form. In simplest terms, this means that anyone can download and run the free and open-source software required to participate in the Bitcoin protocol.

As a Bitcoin user, all you need to know to send Bitcoin to someone else is their Bitcoin address (a series of letters and numbers, not their name or any personal information!). By sending your Bitcoin to an address, what you are doing is broadcasting your transaction (Hi, I'm Alice sending 1 BTC to Bob!) across the Bitcoin network using blockchain technology (more about that below). Since the Bitcoin network has the most up-to-date ledger tracking Alice's wallet balance, the system checks her wallet balance (i.e., Alice has 2 BTC in her wallet, so a transaction of 1 BTC to Bob is valid), and then completes the transaction.

In summary, Bitcoin works by ensuring that this shared ledger always tallies up, and that new Bitcoin transactions (Bob sends 2 BTC back to Alice. Go Alice!) are validated, recorded and then added to the ledger in order. That is the heart of blockchain technology, where new "blocks of information" are added to the chain of blocks that already exist.

How Does Bitcoin Mining Work?

"Mining" refers to the act of adding new blocks to the

blockchain. In simple terms, Bitcoin miners dedicate significant amounts of computing power to solve a cryptographic problem, which is basically a very complex puzzle. The successful miner that solves the puzzle before all the other miners gets rewarded with a "block reward," which is an allocation of a predetermined number of Bitcoin. In some cases, the block rewards are awarded to mining pools, when miners group together to share resources.

Once the puzzle is solved, the block is "confirmed," and it is added to the blockchain. This new information is sent to all nodes, aka participants in the Bitcoin protocol, and the shared ledger is updated once again.

As Bitcoin's price rises, the block reward becomes increasingly more attractive. This incentivizes more miners to join in the competition to mine for blocks. In return, the more miners there are in the system, the more secure the network is. In addition, the increased competition also means miners are continually investing in newer hardware to ensure their computing power remains relevant for the fight for block rewards.

What Is a Bitcoin Halving?

To ensure that the value of Bitcoin is not compromised by an infinite supply, Satoshi Nakamoto wrote in a "halving event" that happens every 210,000 blocks. When Bitcoin's network first began, Bitcoin's block reward was 50 BTC per block mined. This was halved in 2012, at block #210,000, where the block reward became 25 BTC. The second halving was in 2016, at block #420,000, and the block reward became 12.5 BTC.

This process will continue every 210,000 blocks, until the total supply of BTC (21 million BTC) has been reached. It is estimated that the final block reward will be paid in 2140!

How Can I Store my Bitcoin?

There are many different ways of storing your Bitcoin – here's just a few:

1. Keep it on a Bitcoin exchange

There are many Bitcoin different exchanges all over the world. All of these exchanges allow you to sell Bitcoin for other cryptocurrencies (altcoins) or government currencies (USD, EUR, GBP etc.) At the same time, these Bitcoin exchanges allow you to store your BTC with them, which means that the burden of keeping it safe is on them. Do note that incidents have occurred when exchanges have been hacked or lost their customers' BTC, so do your own research when you're looking for an exchange that's safe to hold your cryptoassets.

2. Keep it in a Bitcoin wallet

Instead of keeping it on a Bitcoin exchange, you could keep your Bitcoin in a Bitcoin wallet instead. Wallets come in two forms — hot and cold. Hot wallets are software that stays connected to the internet, aka storing your Bitcoin online. It is more convenient to transact via a hot wallet, but they logically are more susceptible to being attacked, as they stay connected to the internet.

Cold wallets are wallets that are not "online." They are less prone to attack, as hackers cannot access this type of cold storage via the internet, but they are also a lot less convenient for the user as they may be cost-prohibitive and require more technical understanding to operate. Examples of cold wallets are hardware wallets and paper wallets.

ABOUT ETHEREUM

What Is Ethereum?

Ethereum is a smart contract platform that enables developers to build decentralized applications (DApps) on its blockchain. Ether (ETH) is the native digital currency of the Ethereum platform.

Ethereum is supported in part by the Ethereum Foundation, a non-profit that is part of the larger Ethereum ecosystem including enterprise Ethereum consortiums like the Ethereum Enterprise Alliance.

How Does Ethereum Work?

Vitalik Buterin first conceptualized Ethereum in 2013 with the idea of developing an open-source blockchain platform different from Bitcoin (BTC), thus pioneering smart contracts. On the Ethereum blockchain, a smart contract behaves like a self-operating computer program that automatically executes when specific conditions are met. Blockchain allows smart contracts' code to be run exactly as programmed without any possibility of downtime, censorship, fraud or third-party interference.

The Ethereum network went live on July 30, 2015, with 73 million Ether pre-mined.

How Do You Mine Ethereum?

Ethereum mining is currently based on a proof-of-work (PoW) protocol (like Bitcoin), with future plans to switch to proof-of-stake. Ethereum mining works when miners use their computational power to solve a mathematical problem (finding the hash of a block's unique header metadata). The first miner to success-fully solve the problem (find the hash) then broadcasts that the block has been mined to the entire Ethereum network for other nodes to validate and add the block to the blockchain.

The Ethereum blockchain was supposed to migrate from a PoW system to the less energy-investive proof-of-stake system (PoS) system in January 2020, but the deadline was not met. A switch to PoS and the release of Ethereum 2.0 is still expected for later in 2020.

Ethereum mining is based on the Ethash algorithm, and ETH miners originally received a block reward of 5 ETH per block when the network first went live. In the end of 2017, the Byzan-tine hard fork of the Ethereum blockchain lowered the block re-wards from 5 ETH to 3 ETH. In early 2019, the reward was again lowered to 2 ETH in what is known as "the thirdening."

The Ethash proof-of-work protocol makes it not profitable to use ASICs to mine (unlike Bitcoin). Each Ethereum block aims to take an average of 12 seconds to be mined, and the level of diffi-culty of mining is proportional to the total amount of computer power (or network's hashrate) being used to mine Ethereum.

Ethereum transactions are called "gas" and they are respon-sible for powering operations on the entire network, meaning you have to spend your "gas" (Ether) in order to make changes to the blockchain. Ethereum also has a Turing complete internal code.

What Is Ethereum Used For?

The Ethereum platform is used by developers to build new kinds of DApps, which can have a variety of uses ranging from the creation of new digital assets and uncensorable web apps to building decentralized autonomous organizations and more. Anyone around the world is able to freely connect to the Ethereum network.

Ether, the native currency of the Ethereum blockchain, is also used as digital money and can be sent to anyone in the world instantly. Ether can be used as a form of payment or a store of value.

ABOUT TETHER

Tether (USDT) is a cryptocurrency with a value meant to mirror the value of the U.S. dollar. The idea was to create a stable cryptocurrency that can be used like digital dollars. Coins that serve this purpose of being a stable dollar substitute are called "stable coins." According to their site, Tether converts cash into digital currency, to anchor or "tether" the value of the coin to the price of national currencies like the US dollar, the Euro, and the Yen. Tether (USDT) is issued on the Omni, TRON, and ETH blockchains.

ABOUT XRP

What Is XRP?

To begin with, it's important to understand the difference between XRP, Ripple and RippleNet. XRP is the currency that runs on a digital payment platform called RippleNet, which is on top of a distributed ledger database called XRP Ledger. While RippleNet is run by a company called Ripple, the XRP Ledger is open-source and is not based on blockchain, but rather the previously mentioned distributed ledger database.

The RippleNet payment platform is a real-time gross settlement (RTGS) system that aims to enable instant monetary transactions globally. While XRP is the cryptocurrency native to the XRP Ledger, you can actually use any currency to transact on the platform.

While the idea behind the Ripple payment platform was first voiced in 2004 by Ryan Fugger, it wasn't until Jed McCaleb and Chris Larson took over the project in 2012 that Ripple began to be built (at the time, it was also called OpenCoin).

How Does XRP Work?

XRP was created by Ripple to be a speedy, less costly and more scalable alternative to both other digital assets and existing monetary payment platforms like SWIFT.

RippleNet's ledger is maintained by the global XRP Community, with Ripple the company as an active member. The XRP Ledger processes transactions roughly every 3-5 seconds, or whenever independent validator nodes come to a consensus on both the order and validity of XRP transactions — as opposed to proof-of-work mining like Bitcoin (BTC). Anyone can be a Ripple validator, and the list is currently made up of Ripple along with universities, financial institutions and others.

How Do You Store XRP?

You can either store your XRP on an exchange, where the exchange is responsible for the safety of your asset, or store your XRP in a cold or hot wallet.

ABOUT CHAINLINK

What Is Chainlink?

Chainlink (LINK) is a decentralized oracle network which aims to connect smart contracts with data from the real world. Chainlink was developed by Sergey Nazarov, with Steve Ellis as the other co-founder. It held an ICO in September 2017, raising $32 million, with a total supply of 1 billion LINK tokens. LINK, the cryptocurrency native to the Chainlink decentralized oracle network, is used to pay node operators. Since the Chainlink network has a reputation system, node providers that have a large amount of LINK can be rewarded with larger contracts, while a failure to deliver accurate information results in a deduction of tokens. Developers describe LINK as "an ERC20 token, with the additional ERC223 'transfer and call' functionality of transfer (address, uint256, bytes), allowing tokens to be received and processed by contracts within a single transaction." Following the 2017 $32 million LINK ICO, 32 percent of LINK tokens were sent to node operators to incentivize the ecosystem and 30 percent stayed within Chainlink for development (35 percent were sold in the public token sale).

What Are Oracles?

Chainlink is a platform that aims to bridge the gap between blockchain technology-based smart contracts (made widespread by Ethereum), and real world applications. Since blockchains cannot access data outside their network, oracles (a defi instrument) are needed to function as data feeds in smart contracts. In Chainlink's case, the oracles are connected to the Ethereum network. Oracles provide external data (e.g. temperature, weather) that trigger smart contract executions upon the fulfillment of predefined conditions. Participants on the Chainlink network are incentivized (through rewards) to provide smart contracts with access to external data feeds like API information. Should users desire access to off-chain data, they can submit a requesting contract to Chainlink's network. These contracts will match the requesting contract with the appropriate oracles. The contracts include a reputation contract, an order-matching contract and an aggregating contract. The aggregating contract gathers data of the selected oracles to find the most accurate result.

ABOUT BITCOIN CASH

What is Bitcoin Cash?

Bitcoin Cash is a peer-to-peer electronic cash system that aims to become sound global money with fast payments, micro fees, privacy, and high transaction capacity (big blocks). In the same way that physical money, such as a dollar bill, is handed directly to the person being paid, Bitcoin Cash payments are sent directly from one person to another.

As a permissionless, decentralized cryptocurrency, Bitcoin Cash requires no trusted third parties and no central bank. Unlike traditional fiat money, Bitcoin Cash does not depend on monetary middlemen such as banks and payment processors. Transactions cannot be censored by governments or other centralized corporations. Similarly, funds cannot be seized or frozen — because financial third parties have no control over the Bitcoin Cash network.

What is Bitcoin Cash used for?

Bitcoin Cash combines gold-like scarcity with the spendable nature of cash. With a limited total supply of 21 million coins, Bitcoin Cash is provably scarce and, like physical cash, can be easily spent. Transactions are fast with transaction fees typically less than a tenth of a cent. Anybody can accept Bitcoin Cash payments with a smartphone or computer.

Bitcoin Cash has various use cases. In addition to peer-to-peer payments between individuals, Bitcoin Cash can be used to pay participating merchants for goods and services in-store and online. Very low fees enable new micro-transaction economies, such as tipping content creators and rewarding app users a few cents. Bitcoin Cash also reduces the fees and settlement times for remittances and cross-border trade. Other use cases include tokens, simplified smart contracts, and private payments with tools such as CashShuffle and CashFusion.

Is Bitcoin Cash different from Bitcoin?

In 2017, the Bitcoin project and its community split in two over concerns about Bitcoin's scalability. The result was a hark fork which created Bitcoin Cash, a new cryptocurrency considered by supporters to be the legitimate continuation of the Bitcoin project as peer-to-peer electronic cash. All Bitcoin holders at the time of the fork (block 478,558) automatically became owners of Bitcoin Cash.

Unlike Bitcoin BTC, Bitcoin Cash aims to scale so it can meet the demands of a global payment system. At the time of the split, the Bitcoin Cash block size was increased from 1MB to 8MB. An increased block size means Bitcoin Cash can now handle significantly more transactions per second (TPS) while keeping fees extremely low, solving the issues of payment delays and high fees experienced by some users on the Bitcoin BTC network.

Development to further optimize the Bitcoin Cash network continues on the Bitcoin Cash roadmap, led by the Bitcoin ABC full node team. Planned upgrades take place every six months to put into effect the latest network developments.

How do you mine Bitcoin Cash?

Mining is the process in which new Bitcoin Cash transactions are confirmed and new blocks are added to the Bitcoin Cash blockchain. Miners use computing power and electricity to solve complex puzzles. By doing so, they gain the ability to produce new blocks of transactions. If one of their blocks is accepted by the network, the miner, or mining pool, earns a block reward in the form of newly-issued Bitcoin Cash.

Mining is highly competitive. As the price of Bitcoin Cash in the marketplace rises, more miners are incentivized to bring more hash rate into the ever-increasing miner competition to produce blocks and have them accepted by the Bitcoin Cash network. More miners make the network more secure by increasing and distributing the hash rate. This prevents a single miner from having control over the network.

Anyone can mine Bitcoin Cash. Mining requires specialized hardware called mining equipment, which can either be bought or rented. Miners also need to run a full node software (with the majority of miners currently running Bitcoin ABC) to build blocks and connect to the rest of the Bitcoin Cash network. Mining can be done independently but miners often pool their hash rate together and share proportionally in the earned block rewards.

ABOUT LITECOIN

What Is Litecoin?

Litecoin is a peer-to-peer cryptocurrency created by Charlie Lee, a former Google employee, in 2011. The cryptocurrency was created based on the Bitcoin protocol, but it differs in terms of the hashing algorithm used, hard cap, block transaction times and a few other factors. Litecoin was released via an open-source client on GitHub on Oct. 7, 2011, and the Litecoin Network went live five days later on Oct. 13, 2011.

Lee's intention behind Litecoin was to create a "lite version of Bitcoin," and its developers have always stated that Litecoin can be seen as the "silver" to Bitcoin's "gold." Litecoin differs from Bitcoin in its prioritization of transaction confirmation speed, which is about 2.5 minutes per block. However, Litecoin users may have to wait up to around 30 minutes for their transaction to be processed due to network congestion.

Litecoin is accepted at a variety of merchants, you can see an updated list on the Litecoin Foundation's website.

How Do You Mine Litecoin?

Unlike Bitcoin, Litecoin uses the memory intensive Scrypt proof of work mining algorithm. Scrypt allows consumer-grade hardware such as GPU to mine those coins, meaning that you can still mine Litecoin on a Mac or on Windows either solo or via a pool, something no longer possible for Bitcoin mining. Scrypt, by design, is more accessible for users that want to mine via CPUs or GPU, as ASIC-based mining rigs are not suitable for Litecoin mining.

In the beginning, Litecoin block rewards were 50 Litecoin, but the block reward was halved in 2015 to 25, and will continue to halve until its hard cap of 84 million Litecoin is reached.

Where Can You Store Litecoin?

Litecoin can be stored like most cryptocurrencies either on an exchange or in a cold or hot storage wallet.

ABOUT BITCOIN SV

What Is Bitcoin SV?

Bitcoin SV (Satoshi's Vision) stems from a hard fork that split Bitcoin Cash into two different digital currencies on Nov. 15, 2018. The hard fork resulted in a hash war that determined how the chains would be split, resulting in Bitcoin SV and Bitcoin ABC. Bitcoin ABC became the dominant chain and took over the BCH ticker, while Bitcoin SV has its own ticker. According to their website, the Bitcoin SV project is primarily backed by CoinGeek Mining with development work by nChain.

Bitcoin SV claims a strict adherence to Satoshi Nakamoto's vision for the original Bitcoin, with the original Bitcoin white paper serving as a core document for the project.

What Is the Difference Between Bitcoin Cash and Bitcoin SV?

Bitcoin Cash and Bitcoin SV split in November 2018 over differences in opinion about proposed technical updates to Bitcoin Cash protocol. Craig Wright and Calvin Ayre disagreed with two updates in particular, Canonical Transaction Ordering (CTOR) and OP_CHECKDATASIG, which would require transactions in blocks to have a specific order and bring smart-contract functionality to Bitcoin Cash, respectively. The opposition to the updates forked the chain in November 2018, raising the block size limit to 128MB.

What Is a Bitcoin SV Halving?

A Bitcoin SV halving is when mining rewards per block will be reduced by 50%. The first Bitcoin SV halving occurred on April 10, 2020, when the block rewards per block mined were reduced from 12.5 to 6.25 Bitcoin SV.

Bitcoin SV, Bitcoin Cash and Bitcoin all have the same 21 million hard cap put forward by Satoshi Nakamoto in his white paper.

Where Can You Store Bitcoin SV?

Bitcoin SV can be stored on any wallet or crypto exchange that has support for the currency.

ABOUT CRYPTO.COM COIN

Crypto.com was founded in 2016 with the goal of accelerating the world's transition to cryptocurrency. Key products include: the Crypto.com Wallet & Card App, a place to buy, sell, and pay with crypto, the MCO Visa Card, a metal card with no annual fees, and the Crypto.com Chain, which reportedly enables users to pay and be paid in crypto, anywhere, for free. Crypto.com is headquartered in Hong Kong with a team size of 120+. For more information, please visit: www.crypto.com

ABOUT BINANCE COIN

What Is Binance Coin (BNB)?

BNB was launched through an initial coin offering in 2017, 11 days before the Binance cryptocurrency exchange went online. It was originally issued as an ERC-20 token running on the Ethereum network, with a total supply capped at 200 million coins, and 100 million BNBs offered in the ICO. However, the ERC-20 BNB coins were swapped with BEP2 BNB on a 1:1 ratio in April 2019 with the launch of the Binance Chain mainnet, and are now no longer hosted on Ethereum.

BNB can be used as a payment method, a utility token to pay for fees on the Binance exchange and for participation in token sales on the Binance launchpad. BNB also powers the Binance DEX (decentralized exchange).

Can You Mine BNB?

You cannot mine BNB as you would a proof-of-work cryptocurrency, since the Binance Blockchain uses the Byzantine Fault Tolerance (BFT) consensus mechanism. Instead, there are validators that earn from securing the network by validating blocks.

What Is a BNB Burn?

Before BNB migrated to Binance Chain, Binance performed coin burns on the Ethereum network using a smart contract burn function. The amount of coins that Binance burns is based on the number of trades of the exchange over three months. Since the Binance Chain launch, BNB coin burns no longer take place on the

Ethereum network and now use a specific command on Binance Chain, as opposed to a smart contract.

ABOUT CARDANO

What Is Cardano?

Cardano (ADA) is a decentralized platform that will allow complex programmable transfers of value in a secure and scalable fashion. Founded by Charles Hoskinson, its development started in 2015, and it then raised around $60 million in an ICO in 2017 before its release. Hoskinson was also one of the founders of Ethereum. Cardano is reportedly the first blockchain platform to evolve out of a scientific philosophy and a research-first driven approach, and one of the first to be built in the Haskell programming language. Cardano is developing a smart contract platform which seeks to deliver more advanced features than any protocol previously developed. The development team consists of a large global collective of expert engineers and researchers. The protocol reportedly features a layered blockchain software stack that is flexible, scalable and is being developed with the most rigorous academic and commercial software standards in the industry. Cardano will use a democratic governance system that allows the project to evolve over time, and fund itself sustainably through a treasury system. Cardano also notes that it will combine users' need for privacy with regulation, so that Cardano's style of regulated computing will foster greater financial inclusion.

Cardano is supported by three organizations that are separate in both ownership and leadership. The Cardano Foundation is an independent, Swiss-based organization that oversees the development of the Cardano ecosystem, IOHK designs and builds Cardano and Emurgo is the for-profit arm that supports Cardano with commercial ventures. Cardano's roadmap for development has been divided into five eras: Byron, Shelley, Goguen, Basho and Voltaire. While each separate era has its own set of functionalities that will be developed and supported in multiple code releases in a sequential order, the development of each era is parallel and simultaneous across the different systems. Cardano also has its own block explorer, which allows users to check the history of ADA transactions that are publicly recorded on the blockchain.

How Do You Mine or Stake Cardano?

Cardano does not run on a proof-of-work blockchain like Bitcoin. Instead, Cardano has a proof-of-stake algorithm known as Ouroboros, which works in a specific way as compared to most proof-of-stake algorithms. Ouroboros divides up time slots called "epochs," which can be compared to working a shift. Each epoch is led by one elected slot leader who is responsible for creating and confirming blocks in the Cardano blockchain. If one slot leader does not create a transaction block in their epoch, the next "shift" leader will try, with a minimum of 50 percent or more of the blocks produced within one epoch. The transactions in the blocks created by slot leaders are then approved by input endorsers, who are elected based on stakes. There can be more than one input endorser in each epoch.

The Ouroboro rewards system has incentives for availability and transaction verification, as opposed to using large amounts of power to mine coins like in proof-of-work. The rewards given for participating in the Cardano blockchain are split between three stakeholders: input endorsers, multiparty computation stakeholders, and slot leaders. Cardano staking is a feature of the Shelley era of the roadmap. The Shelley Incentivized Testnet, live in May 2020, allows ADA holders to earn rewards by either delegating their stakes or running a stake pool.

ABOUT EOS

What Is EOS?

EOSIO blockchain is a decentralized system that is powered by its native cryptocurrency, EOS, and supports decentralized applications (DApps) on its platform. Its native EOS tokens are often used for business purposes and can be used as a "stake" for funding DApps in the EOS ecosystem. Introduced in May 2017 by block.one, EOS does not stand for anything specific, because its creators have never formally defined it. Dan Larimer, who foundedBitshares and Steem, is the CTO of block.one.

EOS initially held a year-long initial coin offering (ICO) in 2017, with a total of 200 million (20% of the tokens) distributed during a five-day period, 700 million more (70%) distributed over the rest of the year and 100 million (10%) held in escrow for block.one.

The EOS protocol acts like Google's Play Store and Apple's App store, emulating most of the attributes of a real computer, including hardware (CPU(s) & GPU(s) for processing, local/RAM memory and hard-disk storage) with the computing resources distributed equally among EOS cryptocurrency holders. EOS also supports a web-toolkit used for interface development.

In essence, EOSIO operates as a smart contract platform and decentralized operating system intended for the deployment of industrial-scale DApps through a decentralized autonomous corporation model. The smart contract platform claims to eliminate transaction fees and also conduct millions of transactions per second. EOS (EOS) is software that introduces a blockchain architecture designed to enable vertical and horizontal scaling of decentralized applications. The EOS software provides accounts, authentication, databases, asynchronous communication and the scheduling of applications across multiple CPU cores and/or clusters.

How Do You Mine EOS?

EOS cannot be mined like proof-of-work cryptocurrencies because it uses a delegated proof-of-stake system; instead, block producers create the blocks and are rewarded for each block by the creation of new EOS tokens. Block producers are disincentivized from giving themselves higher rewards by a limiting mechanism that prevents total annual token supply from increasing more than 5%. EOS token holders also have the power to vote out block producers that they feel are not adhering to the ideals of EOS.

ABOUT TEZOS

What Is Tezos?

Tezos (XTZ) is a multi-purpose platform that supports decentralized applications (DApps) and smart contracts. It was developed by Arthur Breitman, with support from his wife Kathleen Breitman, and launched an initial coin offering (ICO) in 2017 that raised $232 million US dollars. A year after the ICO, Tezos launched its beta network in July 2018.

The Tezos platform aims to combine a self-correcting protocol and on-chain governance to manage network modifications, and supports Turing complete smart contracts.

Tezos is also supported by the Tezos Foundation, which is a Swiss-based entity that promotes the Tezos protocol through grants and other capital vehicles.

How Does Tezos Work?

Tezos works by creating incentives for users to want to participate in the core development of the Tezos protocol. However, the blockchain also uses formal mathematical proofs to ensure that certain critical properties of the Tezos protocol are maintained, thus keeping the network decentralized.

Can You Mine Tezos?

You can't mine on the Tezos blockchain as you would a proof-of-work cryptocurrency like Bitcoin, as it is based instead on a proof-of-stake consensus (DPoS) mechanism rather than on a proof-of-work protocol. The Tezos protocol is powered by XTZ tokens, which are created through "baking."

What Is Tezos Baking?

Instead of mining, Tezos bakers (also known as delegates) earn rewards of Tezos tokens by staking, i.e. they put up deposits and are rewarded for signing and publishing blocks, and witnesses then validate the blocks. Dishonest bakers lose their XTZ deposits, which is an incentive to stay honest in the Tezos ecosystem. Tezos is implemented in the OCaml programming language, which is said to offer "functional, imperative, and object-oriented styles."

ABOUT TRON

What Is TRON?

TRON (TRX) was founded in 2017 by Justin Sun through a Singapore-based non-profit called the Tron Foundation. The Tron Foundation's 2017 initial coin offering (ICO) created 100 billion TRX and raised a total of $70 million.

The TRON Protocol represents the architecture of an operating system based on blockchain technology which could enable developers to create smart contracts and decentralized applications (DApps), freely publish, own and store data and other content. According to the TRON Foundation, the ecosystem surrounding this network specializes in offering massive scalability and consistent reliability capable of processing transactions at a high rate via high-throughput computing. TRON was initially created as a token based on Ethereum, but migrated to its own network in 2018. Holders of ERC20 TRX tokens traded them for the TRX digital currency on the TRON network, and the Ethereum-based tokens were then destroyed.

TRON founder Justin Sun is known for being active on social media. He is also the CEO of BitTorrent, and acquired Steem in 2020.

How Do You Mine TRON?

TRON is based on a delegated proof-of-stake system, unliked Bitcoin's proof-of-work, where a rotating cast of 27 "super representatives" validate the transaction on the blockchain. They are chosen every six hours, blocks are created on the blockchain every three seconds and super representatives receive 32 TRX as a block reward. You can also participate in the TRON blockchain by running a witness node (proposing blocks and voting on protocol decisions), a full node (broadcast transactions and blocks) or a Solidity node (syncs blocks from full nodes, provides APIs).

Users participate in staking on the TRON network by using "Tron Power," a network resource equal to the amount of TRX that is being staked.

ABOUT STELLAR

What Is Stellar?

The Stellar network is an open-source, distributed and community-owned blockchain network used to facilitate cross-asset transfers of value. Stellar aims to facilitate these transfers at a fraction of a penny, while aiming to be an open financial system that gives people of all income levels access to low-cost financial services. The native digital currency of the Stellar network is known as Lumens (XLM). Every Stellar account is required to hold a small amount of Lumens to act as a barrier against spamming the Stellar payments system. Through the use of Lumens, a user can send any currency that they own to anyone else in a different currency. Stellar also supports smart contracts.

Stellar was co-founded by former lawyer Joyce Kim and Jed McCaleb in 2014. Jed McCaleb is also the founder of the now-defunct Mt. Gox exchange, and the co-founder of Ripple. In fact, both payment networks used the same protocol initially. Like Ripple, Stellar is also a payment technology that aims to connect financial institutions and drastically reduce the cost and time required for cross-border transfers, although while Ripple focuses on banks, Stellar focuses on banking the unbanked. One of Stellar's largest partnerships is with IBM — signed in October 2017 — to set up multiple currency corridors for ease of payment in the South Pacific.

Stellar is also supported by the Stellar Development Foundation, a non-profit that helps with the maintenance of Stellar's codebase, and supports Stellar communities, among other things.

How Do You Mine Stellar?

Unlike proof-of-work cryptocurrencies like Bitcoin, Stellar can't be mined. When the Stellar network went live in 2014, 100 billion Lumens were created with a 1% annual inflation rate. However, in October 2019, a community vote ended the inflation mechanism, and the overall lumen supply was reduced in November 2019, leaving the total supply at around 50 billion Lumens with no more Lumens to be created. While around 20 billion Lumens are in the open market, the Stellar Development Foundation has the other 30 billion, which it uses to support the Stellar ecosystem, but those Lumens will also gradually enter the open market.

ABOUT MONERO

What Is Monero?

Monero (XMR) is a private, secure and untraceable cryptocurrency that was launched April 18, 2014 as a fork of ByteCoin. It is an open-source, privacy-oriented digital currency built on a blockchain that is designed to be opaque. With Monero, it is said you are in complete control of your funds and privacy, as no one else can see anyone else's balances or transactions.

Monero works as a privacy-oriented cryptocurrency by using ring signatures and stealth addresses. A ring signature is an anonymous digital signature that does not reveal who signed the transaction. They are generated on the Monero platform through a combination of a sender's account keys and public keys on the blockchain. Stealth addresses are randomly-generated addresses that are created during each transaction for a one-time use, and they hide a transaction's destination address, as well as the receiver's identity. Ring confidential transactions (RingCT) also hides the amount of the transaction; this feature was added in January 2017 as a mandatory feature of all Monero network transactions.

Monero is based on the CryptoNote protocol, and has a dynamic block size and fees, as opposed to Bitcoin.

How Do You Mine Monero?

Monero mining can be done solo or by joining a mining pool. Unlike some proof-of-work cryptocurrencies like Bitcoin, mining Monero does not require application-specific integrated circuits (ASICs), even though it is based on a proof-of-work algorithm. Monero mining can be done on any CPU or GPU, on a Windows, Mac, Linux and Android, as the Monero mining algorithm specifically supports "little" nodes.

A popular Monero miner, Coinhive, shut down in March 2019. The service had worked by generating a Monero mining script as an alternative to advertisements, as website visitors' CPU would be used to mine Monero, with the site getting a percentage of Monero mined in the place of ad revenue.

How Do You Use Monero?

Monero is used as a cryptocurrency that offers a high level of anonymity and privacy.

ABOUT NEO

Neo describes itself as an open-source platform driven by the community. It utilizes blockchain technology and digital identities to digitize and automate the management of assets using smart contracts. Using a distributed network, it aims to create a smart economy by building infrastructures of the next-gen Internet and creating a solid foundation for mass blockchain adoption. Learn more at (https://neo.org)

ABOUT COSMOS

Cosmos (ATOM) is a cryptocurrency. Cosmos has a current supply of 260,252,107.426. It is currently trading on 144 active markets More information can be found at https://cosmos.network/.

ABOUT USD COIN

USDC is a fully collateralized US dollar stablecoin. It is an Ethereum powered coin and is the brainchild of CENTRE, an open source project bootstrapped by contributions from Circle and Coinbase. USDCs are issued by regulated and licensed financial institutions that maintain full reserves of the equivalent fiat currency in a 1 USDC:1 USD ratio. Issuers are required to report their USD reserve holdings frequently, and Grant Thornton LLP issues reports on those holdings every month.

ABOUT UMA

UMA describes itself as a decentralized financial contracts platform built to enable Universal Market Access—UMA.

ABOUT NEM

NEM (XEM), which stands for New Economy Movement, is a dual-layer blockchain that is written in Java and launched in 2015. The NEM mainnet supports multiple ledgers and has a NEM Smart Asset system, where nodes on the NEM blockchain process API calls. Its native currency is XEM, is 'harvested' using its POI (Proof-of-Importance) algorithm. The 'importance' of NEM users is determined by the number of coins they have and the number of transactions associated with their wallet. NEM also has an encrypted P2P messaging system, multisignature accounts, and an Eigentrust++ reputation system.

ABOUT UNUS SED LEO

UNUS SED LEO (LEO) is a cryptocurrency token and operates on the Ethereum platform. It is currently trading on 26 active markets. More information can be found at https://www.bitfinex.com/.

ABOUT HUOBI TOKEN

Huobi Token (HT) is an exchange based token and native currency of the Huobi crypto exchange. The HT can be used to purchase monthly VIP status plans for transaction fee discounts, vote on exchange decisions, gain early access to special Huobi events, receive crypto rewards from seasonal buybacks and trade with other cryptocurrencies listed on the Huobi exchange.

ABOUT
YEARN.FINANCE

yearn.finance (YFI) is a cryptocurrency token and operates on the Ethereum platform. It is currently trading on 140 active markets. More information can be found at https://yearn.finance/.

ABOUT IOTA

IOTA (IOTA) is a distributed ledger for the Internet of Things that uses a directed acyclic graph (DAG) instead of a conventional blockchain.

Its quantum-proof protocol, Tangle, reportedly brings benefits like 'zero fees, infinite scalability, fast transactions, and secure data transfer'.

The IOTA Tangle is a Directed Acyclic Graph which has no fees on transactions and no fixed limit on how many transactions can be confirmed per second in the network; instead, the throughput grows in conjunction with activity in the network; i.e., the more activity, the faster the network.

ABOUT AAVE

Aave (LEND) is a cryptocurrency token and operates on the Ethereum platform. Aave has a current supply of 1,299,999,941.703. It is currently trading on 134 active markets. More information can be found at https://aave.com/.

ABOUT VECHAIN

VeChain is an enterprise-focused blockchain ecosystem that aims to enhance supply chain management by connecting block-chain technology with the real world through 'a comprehensive governance structure, a robust economic model, and advanced IoT integration'. VeChain enables manufacturers to assign products with unique identifiers on the platform, thereby allowing participants to track the movement and provenance of products in a supply chain. Started in June 2015, VeChain describes itself as 'a pioneer of real-world applications using public blockchain technology, with international operations in Singapore, Luxembourg, Tokyo, Shanghai, Paris, Hong Kong, and San Francisco'

ABOUT DASH

What is Dash?

Since its creation in January 2014, Dash has added features such as:

- Two-tier network with incentivized nodes and decentralized project governance (Masternodes)
- Instantly settled payments (InstantSend)
- Instantly immutable blockchain (ChainLocks)
- Optional privacy (PrivateSend)

How does Dash work?

The Dash Network is governed by masternodes, servers backed by collateral held in Dash designed to provide advanced services securely and governance over Dash's proposal system. In exchange for part of the block reward, masternodes provide a second layer of services to the network. They facilitate functions such as InstantSend, PrivateSend, and ChainLocks, which reportedly protect Dash against 51% mining attacks.

Dash governance system, or treasury, distributes 10% of the block rewards for the development of the project in a competitive and decentralized way. This has allowed the creation of many funded organizations, including Dash Core Group, Inc. (DCG), which supports continued development, integrations, and other activities of Dash.

Within the first 48 hours of Dash's launch, approximately 2.0 million coins were mined, which significantly exceeded the planned emission schedule. Dash was originally forked from Litecoin, and although Litecoin suffered a similar issue at its launch due to a bug in its difficulty adjustment algorithm, this was not widely understood at the time of Dash's launch. Excluding the first two Litecoin blocks (which were mined prior to release), coin emission during the first 24 hours was elevated resulting in the creation of 500,000 Litecoin in the first 24 hours. While it is well-documented that Dash inherited the bug from Litecoin, there has nonetheless been widespread speculation about whether the resulting fastmine was intentional to benefit early miners.

Many individuals competed for block rewards at launch, similar to other projects launching at that time. In the subsequent years, Dash has been actively traded on exchanges through several market cycles, which today makes it one of the most well-distributed cryptocurrencies, according to Google Cloud.

ABOUT ZCASH

Launched in 2016 by Zooko Wilcox-O'Hearn and based on the Zerocoin protocol, Zcash (ZEC) is a decentralized and open-source privacy-focused cryptocurrency that enables selective transparency of transactions. Zcash transactions can either be transparent or shielded through a zero-knowledge proof called zk-SNARKs. This allows the network to maintain a secure ledger of balances without disclosing the parties or amounts involved. Instead of publishing spend-authority and transaction values, the transaction metadata is encrypted and zk-SNARKs are used to prove that nobody is being dishonest.

ABOUT ETHEREUM CLASSIC

Ethereum Classic is a decentralized blockchain platform that lets anyone build and use decentralized applications that run on blockchain technology. Like Bitcoin, no one controls or owns Ethereum Classic – it is an open-source project built by people around the world. Ethereum Classic was designed to be adaptable and flexible, with the goal of making it easy to create new applications on the Ethereum Classic platform

ABOUT MAKER

Maker is a smart contract platform on the Ethereum chain that backs and stabilizes the value of stablecoin DAI through a dynamic system of Collateralized Debt Positions (CDP), autonomous feedback mechanisms, and appropriately incentivized external actors. MKR tokens are created or destroyed in accordance with price fluctuations of the DAI coin in order to keep it as close to $1 USD as possible, and is part of a fully inspectable system on the Ethereum blockchain. MKR tokens are also used to pay transaction fees on the Maker system, and provides holders with voting rights within Maker's continuous approval voting system.

ABOUT OMG NETWORK

OMG Network (first developed as OmiseGO) is a non-custodial, Layer 2 scaling solution for transferring value on Ethereum. How the protocol processes transactions is centralized, but its Plasma-based design aims to decentralize network security. It also relies on Ethereum at its final arbitration layer. Most blockchain ecosystems are limited by low throughput, high and unpredictable transaction fees, and poor user experience. The project's team believes these are barriers that need to be overcome before businesses and developers will adopt blockchain for real-world applications, leading them to develop the OMG Network.

The core security proposition of Plasma revolves around honest users being able to exit the child chain (in other words, withdraw funds to the root chain) at any time. To exit the child chain, a user submits an exit transaction – along with an exit bond – to the root chain. The exit is subject to a "challenge period," during which any user can prove, if applicable, that the exit is invalid. If successfully shown to be invalid, the exit is not processed, and the challenger is awarded the exit bond. This exit game is solely dependent on the root chain.

As the child chain relies on the root chain to be its ultimate arbiter, it must periodically commit a hashed version of its state changes to the root chain by way of a smart contract. As opposed to submitting individual transaction data onto the root chain, the child chain bundles transactions into a Merkle tree and submits the root hash. Beyond these core elements, there is no prescribed configuration for a Plasma chain. They can take on different consensus protocols, block validation mechanisms, or fraud proofs. The design is adaptable to the use case. OMG Network is based on the Plasma MoreVP design, an extension of Minimum Viable Plasma optimized for the settlement of payments and value exchange between users and exchanges.

The original OMG Network team (under the OmiseGO name) co-authored the original Plasma white paper with Joseph Poon and was also the first project to perform an airdrop, a way to more widely share ownership of our token with the existing Ethereum community.

ABOUT SYNTHETIX NETWORK TOKEN

What is Synthetix?

Synthetix is a derivatives liquidity protocol on Ethereum that enables the issuance and trading of synthetic assets. Each synthetic asset (or Synth) is an ERC20 token which tracks the price of an external asset; for example, each sUSD token tracks the price of the US dollar (and unlike the other synthetic assets, is fixed at 1). A wide variety of Synths exists within Synthetix, including fiat currencies, cryptocurrencies, commodities, and inverse indexes. In principle, the system can support any asset with a clear price and provides on-chain exposure to an unlimited range of real-world assets. The protocol will enable a variety of trading features including binary options, futures, and more.

How does Synthetix work?

Synthetix is otherwise composed of a smart contract infrastructure and a set of incentives that maintains Synth prices. It is underpinned by the value of the Synthetix Network Token (SNX). SNX acts as collateral; staking a proportional value of SNX is required to mint Synths. Stakers are rewarded for supporting the system with a pro-rata share of the fees generated by activity in the system. The value of SNX is thus directly connected with the usage of the network it collateralizes.

This mechanism allows Synthetix to support instantaneous, near-frictionless conversion between different flavors of Synths without the liquidity and slippage issues experienced by other decentralized exchanges. The resulting network of tokens supports an extensive set of use cases including trading, loans, payments, remittance, eCommerce, and more.

Synthetix was launched in late 2017, originally under the name of Havven (HAV).

ABOUT ONTOLOGY

Ontology describes itself as a provider of high-performance public blockchains, which includes distributed ledger and smart contract systems.

The Ontology blockchain framework reportedly supports public blockchain systems that can be customized for different applications. Ontology supports collaboration among chain networks with its various protocol groups.

Ontology aims to constantly provide common modules on the underlying infrastructure for different kinds of distributed scenarios, such as those for the distributed digital identity framework and distributed data exchange protocol. Ontology intends to continue developing new common modules based on specific scenario requirements.

Ontology uses a dual token (ONT and ONG) model. ONT is a coin and can be used for staking in consensus, whereas ONG is a utility token used for on-chain services. ONT releases ONG periodically.

ABOUT COMPOUND

Compound (COMP) is an ERC-20 asset that powers the community governance of the Compound protocol; COMP tokenholders and their delegates debate, propose, and vote on changes to the protocol.

By placing COMP directly into the hands of users and applications, an increasingly large ecosystem will be able to upgrade the protocol, and will be incentivized to collectively steward the protocol into the future with good governance.

ABOUT CELO

Celo describes itself as an open platform that makes financial tools accessible to anyone with a mobile phone. The Celo Platform is decentralized, programmable, and customizable. It aims to enable a robust ecosystem of organizations, validators, and developers, to build an open financial system that helps their communities grow and prosper.

ABOUT REN

Ren is an open protocol meant to enable the permissionless and private transfer of value between any blockchain. Ren's core product, RenVM, is focused on bringing interoperability to decentralized finance (DeFi).

ABOUT BASIC ATTENTION TOKEN

Led by Brendan Eich (creator of JavaScript and co-founder of Mozilla), Basic Attention Token (BAT) project is an open-source, decentralized ad exchange platform built on the Ethereum platform. The project seeks to address fraud and opaqueness in digital advertising.

The token aims to correctly price user attention within the platform. Advertisers pay BAT to website publishers for the attention of users. The BAT ecosystem includes Brave, an open-source, privacy-centered browser designed to block trackers and malware. It leverages blockchain technology to anonymously and track user attention securely and rewards publishers accordingly.

ABOUT HEDGETRADE

HedgeTrade aims to become a platform where the world's best traders share their knowledge. Traders post predictions into a smart contract-powered Blueprint that users can purchase or unlock in order to access. Traders are rewarded if the Blueprint is correct otherwise the user's purchase is refunded. HedgeTrade aims to revolutionize social trading using blockchain technology.

ABOUT DAI

Dai is decentralized and backed by collateral. The Maker Protocol, which allows anyone anywhere in the world to generate Dai, aims to facilitate greater security, transparency, and trust.

ABOUT BITTORRENT

BitTorrent aims to tokenize the decentralized file-sharing protocol with their cryptocurrency asset launched early in 2019. BTT represents a TRC-10 utility token based on the TRON blockchain that could allow content creators to connect with their audience, earn and spend digital currency without a middleman.

According to their website, BitTorrent (BTT) tokens can be bid in exchange for faster downloads or stored in a wallet built into the BitTorrent client. Both BitTorrent and parent company TRON share a vision of a decentralized internet without barriers.

According to the team, the BitTorrent Protocol is the largest decentralized protocol in the world with over 1 billion users. The Protocol was developed and since maintained by BitTorrent company. Among the various forms of implementations, BitTorrent and μTorrent remain the most popular.

On July 24, 2018, TRON completed the acquisition of the P2P downloading network BitTorrent and all its products. After the acquisition, BitTorrent/uTorrent has successively launched a number of decentralized products, including BitTorrent Speed, BitTorrent File System (BTFS), TronTV, and the newly-joined blockchain live-streaming platform DLive. The team aims to gradually form a strong-related product matrix and provide the best service for users of the BitTorrent community.

ABOUT 0X

0x (ZRX) is an open-source protocol that provides smart contract infrastructure and liquidity to enable the peer-to-peer exchange of tokens on the Ethereum blockchain. ZRX is the token that allows 0x users to vote on Improvement Proposals that evolve the system over time. ZRX token holders can also delegate ZRX to market maker staking pools to earn protocol liquidity rewards (in ETH).

For more info about the ZRX token, visit the official portal.

- ZRX Portal: (https://0x.org/zrx)

ABOUT THETA

THETA (THETA) is an open source protocol that powers a decentralized streaming network. It will allow for decentralized apps (DApps) to be built on top of the platform to enable use cases that span esports, entertainment, and peer-to-peer streaming. SLIVER.tv's DApp was the first application built on the Theta network leveraging its existing user base of millions of esports viewers. In Nov 2018, Tencent Games announced a collaboration with SLIVER.tv to bring Theta rewards to Ring of Elysium players. The founding team has a combined 30+ years of experience in the video streaming space with advisors including Steve Chen, Co-Founder of YouTube, and Justin Kan, Co-Founder of Twitch.

ABOUT AMPLEFORTH

Ampleforth describes itself as smart commodity money. It is chain-agnostic and reportedly less-correlated to Bitcoin and other digital assets.

ABOUT FTX TOKEN

FTX is owned by FTX Trading LTD, a company incorporated in Antigua and Barbuda. FTX was incubated by Alameda Research, a cryptocurrency liquidity provider. FTX's leveraged tokens aim to provide a clean, automated way for users to get leverage. FTT is the FTX ecosystem utility token. Holders of FTT reportedly receive benefits such as:

- Weekly buying and burning of fees
- Lower FTX trading fees
- OTC rebates
- Collateral for futures trading
- Socialized gains from the insurance fund

ABOUT DOGECOIN

There are currently 266 markets trading it.

What Is Dogecoin?

Dogecoin (DOGE) is based on the popular "doge" Internet meme and features a Shiba Inu on its logo. The open-source digital currency was created by Billy Markus from Portland, Oregon and Jackson Palmer from Sydney, Australia, and was forked from Litecoin in December 2013. Dogecoin's creators envisaged it as a fun, light-hearted cryptocurrency that would have greater appeal beyond the core Bitcoin audience, since it was based on a dog meme. Tesla CEO Elon Musk posted several tweets on social media that Dogecoin is his favorite coin.

How Do You Mine Dogecoin?

Dogecoin differs from Bitcoin's proof-of-work protocol in several ways, one of which is by using Scrypt technology. The altcoin has also a block time of 1 minute, and the total supply is uncapped, which means that there is no limit to the number of Dogecoin that can be mined. You can mine Dogecoin either solo, or by joining a mining pool. A Doge miner can mine the digital currency on Windows, Mac or Linux, and with a GPU. As of 2014, you can also mine Litecoin in the same process of mining Dogecoin, as the processes were merged.

What Can Dogecoin Be Used For?

Dogecoin has been used primarily as a tipping system on Reddit and Twitter to reward the creation or sharing of quality content. You can get tipped Dogecoin by participating in a community that uses the digital currency, or you can get your Dogecoin from a Dogecoin faucet. A Dogecoin faucet is a website that will give you a small amount of Dogecoin for free as an introduction to the currency, so that you can begin interacting in Dogecoin communities.

ABOUT ALGORAND

What is Algorand?

Algorand is a scalable, secure, and decentralized digital currency and transactions platform.

Founded by Turing award winner and MIT professor Silvio Micali, Algorand is a permissionless pure proof-of-stake blockchain protocol. Unlike first-generation consensus mechanisms, Algorand's technology finalizes blocks in seconds and provides immediate transaction finality while preventing forks. Algorand does also not reward validators with newly minted tokens.

With a primary focus on developers and their needs, Algorand's node repository has been open-sourced and is publicly available. Algorand provides a robust set of developer tools, DApp analytics through a partnership with Flipside Crypto, and has a number of partners building on their blockchain, including OTOY, Syncsort, TOP Networks, Asset Block and more.

- Maximum Supply (# or Uncapped): 10,000,000,000
- Genesis Block / Distribution Date: June 11, 2019
- Consensus Mechanism (Precise): Permissionless, Pure Proof of Stake
- Emission Type (Precise): Fixed supply with Pre-minted rewards
- Block Time (Seconds): Sub 5 seconds

How does Algorand work?

The Algorand blockchain network has its own official native cryptocurrency, called the Algo, to drive the borderless economy and the system of incentives. The Foundation holds Algos to contribute to the stability of the Algorand blockchain, to incentivize network participation, and to support the Algorand community, ecosystem building, and research. The Algos enter the ecosystem via various channels including development and research grants, participation rewards, and sales. All such activities are disclosed with full transparency to the Algorand community.

Algorand Technology: Algorand utilizes a Pure Proof of Stake, where validators are not rewarded nor are they at risk of being slashed. It becomes impossible for the minority to cheat and irrational for the majority to cheat the system as it would devalue their holdings. There is also no locking of tokens so a user has their tokens available at all time. Blocks are created in two phases where a single token is selected randomly and its owner proposes the next block. Subsequently, 1000 random tokens are selected with their owners then approving the block proposed by the first user.

These phases are ensured by the core protocol called Binary Byzantine Agreement, or Byzantine Agreement ★ ('Star'), encompassing the following advancements:

- Cryptographic sortition (self-selection) To prevent an adversary from targeting committee members, BA★ uses verifiable random functions (VRFs) to randomly select committee members in a private and non-interactive way.
- Participant replaceability. BA★ mitigates adversary targeting a committee member by requiring committee members to speak just once, thus becoming irrelevant to BA★.

Experimental results running on 1,000 Amazon EC2 VMs demonstrate that Algorand can:

- Confirm a 1 MByte block of transactions in ~22 seconds with 50,000 users
- Latency remains nearly constant when scaling to half a million users
- Achieve 125X the transaction throughput of Bitcoin

- Achieve acceptable latency even in the presence of actively malicious users.

A test network for the protocol was launched in July 2018, and the first open-source code was released on Github in October 2018. As such, Algorand encourages anyone to audit its version of the VRF, forked, and extended from the libsodium cryptographic library.

ABOUT TRUEUSD

TrueUSD is a USD-pegged stablecoin, that provides its users with regular attestations of escrowed balances, full collateral and legal protection against the misappropriation of the underlying USD. TrueUSD is issued by the TrustToken platform, the platform that has partnered with registered fiduciaries and banks that hold the funds backing the TrueUSD tokens. The USD funds are regularly verified in scheduled attestations, and kept in third party escrow accounts such that TrustToken has no direct access to the funds.

ABOUT WAVES

Waves Platform's mission lies in creating an ecosystem that aims to accelerate the shift from centralized to decentralized systems and an emphasis on the individual's control of their own funds and assets, personal data, and privacy. Waves Platform describes itself as an open network for Web 3.0 applications and custom decentralized solutions, with a range of purpose-designed tools for making the process of developing and running dApps easy and accessible. Launched in 2016, Waves has since released several blockchain-based solutions. Waves' technology is designed to address the needs of developers and companies that want to leverage the properties of blockchain systems – including their security, auditability, verifiability and the trustless execution of transactions and business logic.

Waves Platform claims to provide everything required to support the backend of Web 3.0 services. In 2017, Waves launched its mainnet with LPoS, decentralized exchange DEX, and later the Waves-NG protocol. In 2018, the Waves development team delivered the first implementation of smart contracts. This was followed by the release of the RIDE programming language in 2019, Strightforward, Predictible and Failproof language for programming logic. In June 2019 the mainnet of Waves Enterprise, a global private blockchain solution, was launched. All of this is complemented with a broad infrastructure: an IDE for sandbox development, tools, SDKs, libraries, frameworks, and protocols for convenient and easy integrations.

Waves Platform consists of three core layers:

Protocol layer: LPoS, Waves-NG, fixed fees, easy mining start, various transactions models

Infrastructure layer: Keeper for private key management, IDE for sandbox development, smart-contracts programming language RIDE and other tools for dApp development, API's, libraries, tools, and frameworks.

Application layer: basic core open-source apps (decentralized exchange, mobile apps, and voting) and various dApps running on the network.

ABOUT NXM

Nexus Mutual uses Ethereum so that people can pool risk together without the need for an insurance company.

ABOUT ENERGY WEB TOKEN

Energy Web Token (EWT) is the native token of the Energy Web Chain, a public, Proof-of-Authority Ethereum Virtual Machine blockchain specifically designed to support enterprise-grade applications in the energy sector. The Energy Web Chain is operated and governed by over 25 Validator nodes from 15 countries, including utilities, grid operators, and startups. In addition to its native token, the EW Chain supports all ERC standards. The Energy Web Chain was launched in June 2019 by Energy Web Foundation - a global nonprofit unleashing blockchain's potential in the energy sector - and its global consortium of Members that includes upstream energy companies, utilities, grid operators, software developers, and technology vendors. For more information, visit energyweb.org.

ABOUT DIGIBYTE

What Is DigiByte?

DigiByte is an open-source blockchain, created in 2013 and released in early 2014 by DigiByte founder Jared Tate. Its network is based on three layers: smart contracts, decentralized applications (DApps) and customizable tokens. The middle layer, the public ledger, is where DigiByte digital assets exist in the network, while the third and bottom later hosts the decentralized nodes, the client software and their communication. A unique factor of DigiByte is its five mining algorithms — Sha256, Scrypt, Skein, Qubit and Odocrypt — whose advanced difficulty adjustment aims to keep the blockchain secure and protect it from malicious attacks. DigiByte has its own block explorer, DigiExplorer. DigiByte was the first major altcoin to activate Segwit in April 2017.

In May 2019, DigiByte launched DigiAssets, which is a scalable second-layer solution on top of the DigiByte blockchain that offers the decentralized issuance of assets, smart contracts, digital identity and other features.

Where Can You Mine DigiByte?

DigiByte is only created through mining, as no tokens were created at its launch. It has a limit of 21 billion coins, which will all be mined by 2035. You can mine DigiByte solo or in a pool, using one of its five mining algorithms.

What Is DigiByte Used For?

DigiByte can be used as a payment method, like a fiat currency, or a store of value. DigiByte coins are also similar to gas in Ethereum in that they run the DigiAsset smart contract network. DigiByte can be stored on an exchange, or in a DigiByte wallet.

ABOUT KYBER NETWORK

Kyber Network's on-chain liquidity protocol allows decentralized token swaps to be integrated into any application, enabling value exchange to be performed seamlessly between all parties in the ecosystem. Tapping on the protocol, developers can build payment flows and financial apps, including instant token swap services, erc20 payments, and innovative financial dapps - helping to build a world where any token is usable anywhere.

ABOUT OKB

OKB (OKB) is a cryptocurrency token and operates on the Ethereum platform. OKB has a current supply of 300,000,000 with 60,000,000 in circulation. The last known price of OKB is $5.70 USD and is up 0.45% over the last 24 hours. It is currently trading on 56 active market(s) with $92,430,491.166 traded over the last 24 hours. More information can be found at https://www.okex.com/.

ABOUT KUSAMA

Kusama is an early, unaudited, and unrefined release of Polkadot. Kusama aims to serve as a proving ground, allowing teams and developers to build and deploy a parachain or try out Polkadot's governance, staking, nomination, and validation functionality in a real environment.

ABOUT QTUM

Qtum (QTUM) is a Proof-of-Stake (PoS) smart contract block-chain platform and value transfer protocol. In PoS, node oper-ators are rewarded for validating transactions. Qtum is built on Bitcoin's UTXO transaction model, with the added functionality of smart contract execution.

ABOUT ICON

ICON is a decentralized blockchain network focused on inter-operability. With ICON's "blockchain transmission protocol", independent blockchains like Bitcoin and Ethereum can connect and transact with each other. This opens up cross-chain use cases that are impossible without an interoperability layer like ICON.

ICON Network describes itself as a general-purpose blockchain protocol based on the native cryptocurrency ICX that can run smart contracts, adopt the BFT-DPoS (Delegated Proof-of-Stake) consensus protocol, and use an economic-governance protocol called DPoC (Delegated Proof-of-Contribution). The ICON Network is powered by a proprietary blockchain engine called 'loopchain' and has the ability to handle hundreds of transactions per second. The ICON project was started to ensure the integrity and transparency of data shared between institutions and companies, and to move mutual assets on heterogeneous blockchains without a centralized organization. In the long term, ICON Network aims to become an 'interchain' that connects multiple blockchains based on BTP technology.

The ICON blockchain is powered by loopchain, a blockchain engine designed by ICONLOOP. ICONLOOP is responsible for loopchain's government and enterprise adoption in South Korea. Loopchain is the Seoul Metropolitan Government's standard blockchain platform.

ABOUT HYPERION

Hyperion (HYN) is a cryptocurrency token and operates on the Ethereum platform. Hyperion has a current supply of 10,000,000,000. It is currently trading on 10 active markets.. More information can be found at https://www.hyn.space/.

ABOUT FLEXACOIN

Flexacoin describes itself as a digital collateral token for facilitating instant cryptocurrency payments, originally developed to collateralize retail payments on the Flexa network. Flexacoin is designed to mitigate the friction between customers paying with crypto and merchants accepting fiat. Users scan a QR code at the point of sale, and the Flexa Network Protocol (FNP) trades the crypto spent for fiat which is then returned to the merchant.

Flexa returns a percentage of every processed transaction to users. Flexa's FNP uses the ERC 20-compliant token called Flexacoin for transactions and a variety of members-only network incentives. The name "Flexa" is an abbreviation of flexibility, according to the team. Flexa requires no additional hardware at the point of sale and optimizes for seamless payment and receipt for the consumer and merchant.

ABOUT BAND PROTOCOL

Band Protocol is a cross-chain data oracle network that aggregates and connects real-world data and APIs to smart contracts. Blockchains enable immutable storage and deterministic, verifiable computations — however, they cannot securely access data available outside the blockchain networks.

Band Protocol enables smart contract applications such as DeFi, prediction markets, and games to be built on-chain without relying on the single point of failure of a centralized oracle.

BandChain describes itself as a high-performant independent blockchain built specifically for oracle computations including settlement, data sourcing, and aggregation that is secured by delegated proof-of-stake. Developers can create a fully customizable oracle script on BandChain which specifies data sources and APIs to connect to, aggregation methods and security parameters. The creation of scripts is permissionless, allowing for quick iterations and extensive support for any type of data. Decentralized oracle is a key infrastructure to enable decentralized finance and other decentralized applications to operate in the most trustless way possible.

With all oracle computations offloaded to BandChain, smart contracts on any destination blockchain can use Band Protocol to query data on-demand and receive a real-time update. Oracle data queries take between 4-6 seconds by 'batching' transactions with data information to enable instant settlement and also protect end-users from consuming delayed data.

Band Protocol is backed by Sequoia Capital and Binance.

ABOUT SUSHISWAP

SushiSwap claims to be an evolution of #Uniswap with $SUSHI tokenomics. SushiSwap protocol better aligns incentives for network participants by introducing revenue-sharing & network effects to the popular AMM model.

ABOUT ELROND

Elrond describes itself as a new blockchain architecture, designed to bring a 1000-fold cumulative improvement in throughput and execution speed. To achieve this, Elrond introduces two features: Adaptive State Sharding mechanism, and a Proof of Stake (PoS) algorithm, enabling linear scalability with a reportedly fast, efficient, and secure consensus mechanism. Thus, Elrond can reportedly process upwards of 10,000 transactions per second (TPS), with 5-second latency, and negligible cost. It aims to become the backbone of a permissionless, borderless, globally accessible internet economy.

ABOUT DFI.MONEY

The former name of DFI.Money is YFII Finance which is a fork of YFI project with YIP-8 implementation.

ABOUT ARAGON

Aragon (ANT) is a decentralized platform built on the Ethereum network that offers a modularized way to create and manage dApps, cryptoprotocols, and decentralized autonomous organizations (DAO). The ANT ERC-20 token will enable its holders to govern the Aragon Network.

The project is led by Luis Cuende, who was featured on the 'Forbes 30 under 30' category in 'Technology'.

ABOUT PAXOS STANDARD

Paxos Standard (PAX) is a stablecoin that allows users to exchange US dollars for Paxos Standard Tokens to 'transact at the speed of the internet'. It aims to meld the stability of the dollar with blockchain technology. Paxos, the company behind PAX, has a charter from the New York State Department of Financial Services, which allows it to offer regulated services in the cryptoasset space.

ABOUT LOOPRING

Loopring (LRC) is an open protocol for scalable non-custodial exchanges on Ethereum. The Loopring protocol smart contracts and zero-knowledge proof circuits allow the building of high-performance DEXes using a zkRollup construction. This allows for higher throughput and lower settlement costs without sacrificing Ethereum-level security guarantees. LRC token can be staked by holders to earn protocol fees, and by DEXes as a bond to follow protocol-defined behaviour.

ABOUT LISK

Lisk (LSK), founded in early 2016 by Max Kordek and Oliver Beddows and headquartered in Zug, Switzerland, is a blockchain application platform that seeks to make blockchain technology more accessible to the masses. Lisk focuses on user experience, developer support and in-depth documentations. Lisk's SDK kit is written in JavaScript so as to allow developers to easily build blockchain applications on the Lisk blockchain and even deploy their own sidechain linked to the Lisk network. The open source Lisk blockchain platform is powered by Lisk (LSK) tokens and operates under the Delegated Proof of Stake (DPoS) consensus model to allow for its network to be secured by democratically elected delegates.

ABOUT AUGUR

Augur (REP) is meant to harness the wisdom of the crowd through prediction markets on a protocol owned and operated by holders of the Ethereum-based Reputation token. In these markets users are said to be able to bet on the outcomes of events such as company performance, election results or even natural phenomena by purchasing shares that would either support or refute the proposed outcomes of such specified events. By design, the user-created markets could return fees to market participants while automating payouts using software meant to be fair, open to all, and completely decentralized.

ABOUT HEDERA HASHGRAPH

Hedera describes itself as a decentralized public network where developers can build secure, fair applications with near real-time consensus. The platform is owned and governed by a council of global members including Avery Dennison, Boeing, Deutsche Telekom, DLA Piper, FIS (WorldPay), Google, IBM, LG Electronics, Magalu, Nomura, Swirlds, Tata Communications, University College London (UCL), Wipro, and Zain Group.

The Hedera Consensus Service (HCS) acts as a trust layer for any application or permissioned network and allows for the creation of an immutable and verifiable log of messages. Application messages are submitted to the Hedera network for consensus, given a trusted timestamp, and fairly ordered. Use HCS to track assets across a supply chain, create auditable logs of events in an advertising platform, or even use it as a decentralized ordering service.

ABOUT ZILLIQA

Introduced in 2017, Zilliqa (ZIL) is centered around the idea of 'Sharding' and was designed to enhance the scalability of cryptocurrency networks such as Ethereum. Sharding is analogous to the concept of 'divide and conquer', where transactions are divided into smaller groups for miners to perform parallel transactional verification. The upshot of this is the ability to reach consensus more quickly, which would increase the number of transactions in a given period. According to the white paper, transactions speed could scale to approximately 1000x that of Ethereum's network. Zilliqa's high throughput means that developers can focus on fleshing out their ideas rather than worrying about network congestion.

ABOUT ARWEAVE

Arweave aims to make information permanence sustainable. Arweave describes itself as a new type of storage that backs data with sustainable and perpetual endowments, allowing users and developers to store data forever. As a collectively owned hard drive that never forgets, Arweave aims to allow users to remember and preserve valuable information, apps, and history indefinitely. By preserving history, it prevents others from rewriting it.

ABOUT BALANCER

Balancer is an automated market maker, decentralized exchange, and liquidity pool protocol built on Ethereum that allows users to provide liquidity for multiple assets simultaneously. Balancer's BAL token acts as a governance token to help the project set features such as issuance rewards and whitelisted pools for liquidity mining. When users trade, their orders are filled by multiple pools with better pricing and lower slippage.

ABOUT DECRED

Decred is a community-directed cryptocurrency with built-in governance designed with the goal of making it a superior long-term store of value.

Decred's hybrid PoW/PoS consensus mechanism, transparent proposal, voting system, and continually funded treasury was designed to make it secure, adaptable, and sustainable.

Every Decred community member with "skin in the game" - stakeholders, developers, and miners - can vote on the direction of the project. Stakeholders collectively determine the policy, development plan, budget, and consensus rule changes. They also approve the miners' work - effectively aligning interests to ensure the best possible outcome for all.

As it moves towards becoming a Decentralized Autonomous Organization (DAO), Decred is intentionally designed to fund all the parties involved in its governance. Each block reward compensates miners, stakeholders, and the Treasury, which pays contractors who work on Decred.

ABOUT OCEAN PROTOCOL

Ocean Protocol is a tokenized service layer that exposes data, storage, compute and algorithms for consumption with a set of deterministic proofs on availability and integrity that serve as verifiable service agreements. There is staking on services to signal quality, reputation, and ward off Sybil Attacks.

Ocean aims to help users unlock data, particularly for AI. It is designed for scale and uses blockchain technology that allows data to be shared and sold in a safe, secure, and transparent manner.

Ocean Protocol weaves business, technical, and governance frameworks together to allow data and services to be shared and sold, in a secure manner. Ocean Protocol stores metadata, links to data, provides a licensing framework, and has toolsets for pricing. A multitude of data marketplaces can hook into Ocean Protocol to provide "last mile" services to connect data providers and consumers. Ocean Protocol is designed so that data owners cannot be locked-in to any single marketplace. The data owner controls each dataset.

ABOUT RESERVE RIGHTS

The Reserve protocol comprises two tokens: the Reserve token (RSV - a decentralized stablecoin) and the Reserve Rights token (RSR - a cryptocurrency used to facilitate the stability of the Reserve token and confers the cryptographic right to purchase excess Reserve tokens as the network grows). The Reserve movement describes itself as a collection of people who believe that cryptocurrencies can do better than fiat money, and that none of the existing options will be able to scale to global use, maintain stable purchasing power, and not be shut down. The team's goal is to make the most accessible, economically strongest, and most robust-to-attack currency and over time, convince a large portion of the world to replace other currencies with it.

ABOUT BINANCE USD

What is BUSD?

Binance USD (BUSD) is a 1:1 USD-backed stable coin issued by Binance (in partnership with Paxos), Approved and regulated by the New York State Department of Financial Services (NYDFS), The BUSD Monthly Audit Report can be viewed from the official website. Launched on 5 Sep 2019, BUSD aims to meld the stability of the dollar with blockchain technology. It is a digital fiat currency, issued as ERC-20 and supports BEP-2.

BUSD Use Case

Based on the price stability, Stablecoin plays an important role in transactions, payments and settlement, and Decentralised Finance (DeFi).

Here are some of the BUSD use case:

- Transfer your digital dollars (BUSD) anywhere in minutes, with low cost and on the blockchain.
- Trade BUSD on different exchanges and DEX.
- Deposit BUSD to earn an interest rate.
- Pay BUSD as payment for goods and services.
- Use BUSD as collateral and loan asset.
- Use BUSD as cross collateral in Futures.
- Store BUSD on an exchange or in a wallet.

ABOUT SIACOIN

Siacoin (SC) aims to provide an open-source low-cost solution for cloud storage, offering encryption and distribution of files chosen for storage by users across a decentralized network of peers. User-controlled private keys give the assertion that no third parties should have access to or control over data stored on the network. As a result, the cloud storage marketplace made available to users of the Sia blockchain is meant to be highly redundant, completely private, and more affordable than many alternatives.

ABOUT TERRA

Terra aims to build new financial infrastructure that works better for everyone. The network is powered by a family of stablecoins, each pegged to major fiat currencies all algorithmically stabilized by Terra's native token, Luna. Terra's mission is to set money free by building open financial infrastructure.

Luna, as the native staking asset from which the family of Terra stablecoins derive their stability, utility, and value, acts both as collateral for the entire Terra economy and as a staking token that secures the PoS network. Luna can be held and traded as a normal cryptoasset, but can also be staked to accrue rewards in the network generated from transaction fees. Luna can also be used to make and vote on governance proposals.

The family of Terra stablecoins achieve stability through consistent mining rewards with a contracting and expanding money supply. For example, if the system has detected that the price of a Terra currency has deviated from its peg, it applies pressure to normalize the price. Currently, the family of Terra stablecoins include: KRT (Terra stablecoin pegged to Korean Won), UST (Terra stablecoin pegged to US Dollar), MNT (Terra stablecoin pegged to Mongolian Togrog), SDR (Terra stablecoin pegged to IMF SDR), with more being added in the future.

ABOUT BITCOIN GOLD

Bitcoin Gold (BTG) is a fork of Bitcoin that occurred on 24 October 2017 on block 419406. Bitcoin Gold changed Bitcoin's proof-of-work algorithm from SHA256 to Equihash rendering specialized mining equipment obsolete in an attempt to democratize the Bitcoin mining process.

BTG is a cryptocurrency with Bitcoin fundamentals, mined on common GPUs instead of specialty ASICs. ASICs tend to monopolize mining to a few big players, but GPU mining means anyone can mine again - restoring decentralization and independence. GPU mining rewards go to individuals worldwide, instead of mostly to ASIC warehouse owners, recreating network effects that Bitcoin used to have.

BTG aims to extend the crypto space with a blockchain that is closely compatible with Bitcoin (with SegWit and Lightning Network). but without using resources like Bitcoin hashpower or vying for the 'real Bitcoin' title. The team aims to create a welcoming space for new devs and new technologies building on a bitcoin base. As a Friendly Fork, the team aims to offer a coin as easy and familiar to implement as Bitcoin, along with space for new ideas with a view towards creating a thriving economy and ecosystem.

ABOUT SWIPE

Swipe is a multi-asset digital wallet application and Visa debit card that enables users buy, sell, and spend various cryptocurrencies. Swipe utilizes the Ethereum blockchain to operate the Swipe Network.

Swipe uses a two-layer approach for its users to combine off-chain and on-chain function on its platform which is powered by the Swipe Token (SXP). For off-chain usage, supported cryptocurrencies can be instantly converted to fiat and used on point of sale. When the Swipe Network is activated in the platform, users receive a smart contract wallet which uses SXP directly on-chain to perform its functions. As functions are being called on the Swipe Network, 80% of those SXP fees are automatically burned creating a deflationary supply model.

Users may use SXP today in the following ways:

• Currency: When users select SXP as a funding source it may be used on the Swipe Visa card to be converted to Euros and spent at millions of merchants. • Staking: To receive the higher tier cards, discounts, and rewards enhancements, users must stake SXP which is locked on-chain. • Fees: If the Swipe Network is activated within the platform, users are able to use SXP towards all fees on the platform such as conversion fee and withdrawal fees

ABOUT BITCOIN DIAMOND

Bitcoin Diamond (BCD) is a hard fork of Bitcoin. The fork occurring at at block height 495866, implemented changes including a new proof of work algorithm to deter attacks on the network and segregation of transaction signatures from transactions on the chain for additional capacity allowing a greater number of transactions per second on the network as a whole.

ABOUT ENJIN COIN

Since its founding in 2009, Enjin has been deeply involved with the gaming industry. The same year, the company launched a gaming community platform called the Enjin Network and has, according to the team, grown it to more than 20 million users over the course of a decade.

In 2017 following an ICO that raised $18.9 million, Enjin established itself as a blockchain ecosystem developer, building a suite of user-first blockchain products that enable anyone to easily manage, explore, distribute, and integrate blockchain assets.

Built on top of an on-chain infrastructure and comprised of the Enjin Platform, Marketplace, Wallet, Beam, and other tools and services, the Enjin ecosystem aims to enable game industry businesses to increase revenue, gain a competitive edge, and innovate.

Forged in gaming, Enjin's tools and services can also be used by companies of all sizes and industries seeking to create blockchain products or utilize tokenized digital assets as part of their acquisition, retention, engagement, and monetization strategies.

The Enjin ecosystem is fueled by Enjin Coin (ENJ), an Ethereum-based cryptocurrency used to directly back the value of blockchain assets. For more information, visit https://enjin.io.

ABOUT SERUM

Project Serum describes itself as a functional decentralized exchange with trustless cross-chain trading, at the speed and price that customers want. Despite living natively on Solana, it will be interoperable with Ethereum.

ABOUT BITSHARES

Bitshares (BTS), formerly known as ProtoShares, is a peer-to-peer distributed ledger and network that can issue collateralized market-pegged smart coins known as bitAssets. For instance, it can issue crypto-based assets, denominated by "bitAsset", that track real-world markets like the USD, such as the bitUSD. Each smart coin has at least 100% of its value backed by the BitShares' native currency, the BTS, which can be converted at any time at an exchange rate set by a trustworthy price feed. Bitshares was created by Dan Larimer, the co-founder of EOS, Steemit, and Cryptonomex. BitShares also has its own decentralized exchange.

ABOUT BZX PROTOCOL

bZz is a decentralized protocol that enables lending and borrowing for margin trading. The protocol can be integrated into new and existing exchanges, or accessed through the native bZx portal.

ABOUT THORCHAIN

THORChain describes itself as a decentralized liquidity network that allows users to swap assets instantly at manipulation-resistant market prices. Swaps are done through permissionless cross-chain liquidity pools that allow users to stake their assets to earn trading fees. Traders can monitor pool prices and earn by arbitraging back to fair market prices. Projects can reportedly stake their treasuries to give their tokens deep liquidity.

ABOUT RAVENCOIN

Ravencoin (RVN) is an open-source blockchain project that specializes in the creation and peer-to-peer transfer of assets. Ravencoin enables users to create and trade any real-world (e.g. commodities) or digital (e.g. virtual goods) assets on a network. The core developers launched Ravencoin on 3 Jan 2018. The project has some prominent backers: Bruce Fenton, Board Member of The Bitcoin Foundation, advises the team while Overstock has made a multi-million dollar investment into the project.

ABOUT NUMERAIRE

Numeraire (NMR) is a cryptocurrency token and operates on the Ethereum platform. Numeraire has a current supply of 10,979,454.346. It is currently trading on 47 active markets More information can be found at https://numer.ai/.

ABOUT NANO

Launched in 2015, Nano describes itself as an open source, sustainable, and secure next-generation digital currency focused on removing perceived inefficiencies present in existing cryptocurrencies. Designed to solve peer to peer transfer of value, Nano aims to revolutionize the world economy through an ultrafast and fee-less network that is open and accessible to everyone.

Nano is reportedly able to offer fast and feeless transactions due to the Block Lattice - a data structure in which all accounts each have their own blockchain, rather than competing with others on a central chain. Consensus is generated through representative voting, where accounts can freely choose their representative at any time with an update of their account chain, thereby providing more control for users to decide who validates transactions.

Each component of the protocol was created with the long term goals of decentralization and accessibility in mind. By creating a system where representatives are not paid to operate, the incentive to participate in the network is shifted to indirect, operational cost savings. The team claims that this change in incentive model is more efficient and removes one of the factors driving centralization in other systems because participants are not encouraged to interact beyond their direct needs and supporting the network, and thus economies of scale become less critical.

ABOUT SOLANA

Founded by former Qualcomm, Intel, and Dropbox engineers in late-2017, Solana is a single-chain, delegated-Proof-of-Stake protocol whose focus is on delivering scalability without sacrificing decentralization or security.

Core to Solana's scaling solution is a decentralized clock titled Proof-of-History (PoH), built to solve the problem of time in distributed networks where there is not a single, trusted, source of time. By using Verifiable Delay Functions, PoH allows each node to locally generate timestamps with SHA256 computations. This eliminates the need for the broadcasts of timestamps across the network, improving overall network efficiency.

ABOUT STATUS

Status (SNT) is an open source messaging platform and mobile interface built to interact with applications that run on the Ethereum network. The Status network token (SNT) is a utility token that fuels a decentralized push notification market, governance of the Status client, along with curation of user-generated content on the network. The team at Status hopes to promote adoption of the decentralized web while staying true to principles such as liberty, security, privacy, transparency, inclusivity and censorship resistance.

ABOUT
DECENTRALAND

Decentraland (MANA) defines itself as a virtual reality platform powered by the Ethereum blockchain that allows users to create, experience, and monetize content and applications. In this virtual world, users purchase plots of land that they can later navigate, build upon, and monetize. Decentraland uses two tokens: MANA and LAND. MANA is an ERC20 token that must be burned to acquire non-fungible ERC721 LAND tokens.

ABOUT BYTOM

Established in early 2017, the Bytom (BTM) Blockchain project was launched to develop a protocol that could tokenize assets from the physical world and represent them in the digital world on a decentralized network. Aiming to help businesses and individuals to register and exchange assets such as securities, bonds, deeds and various types of information, the Bytom blockchain uses a proof-of-work protocol that designed to enable customized contracts, promote AI technology, and provide unique identifiers for assets following a standardized naming convention.

ABOUT BLOCKSTACK

Blockstack aims to build a new decentralized internet where users own their data and apps run locally. A browser portal would be all that is needed to get started.

ABOUT CURVE DAO TOKEN

CRV is a governance token on the Curve platform with time-weighted voting and value accrual mechanisms.

ABOUT NERVOS NETWORK

The Nervos Network describes itself as an open-source public blockchain ecosystem and collection of protocols. The Nervos CKB (Common Knowledge Base) is the layer 1, proof of work public blockchain protocol of the Nervos Network. It reportedly allows any crypto-asset to be stored with the security, immutability and permissionless nature of Bitcoin while enabling smart contracts and layer 2 scaling. It aims to capture the total network value through its "store of value" crypto-economic design and native token, the CKByte.

ABOUT HUSD

HUSD is an ERC-20 token that is 1:1 ratio pegged with USD. It was issued by Stable Universal, an entity that claims to follow US regulations.

ABOUT KAVA.IO

Kava describes itself as a decentralized financial services platform. Kava's principle product is a DeFi lending platform for cryptocurrencies.

ABOUT JUST

JUST Platform's Governance Token JST will be launched on 05/05/2020 during the Poloniex LaunchBase (Token Sale).

JUST aims to build a fair, decentralized financial system that provides stablecoin lending and governance mechanisms for users around the world. JUST is a two-token system. The first token, USDJ is a stablecoin pegged to the US Dollar at a 1:1 ratio and is generated by collateralizing TRX via JUST's CDP portal. JST, the second token, can be used for paying interest, platform maintenance, participating in governance through voting, and other activities on the JUST platform.

JUST allows all transactions, collateralization, and governance to be transparently executed on-chain. JUST is built on the TRON Network, the largest decentralized application ecosystem, and aims to provide a set of easy-to-use and transparent financial services for all its members.

ABOUT GOLEM

Golem (GNT) is a peer-to-peer decentralized marketplace for computing power. The project aims to be an alternative to centralized cloud service providers with its lower price point and open-source community of developers. The Golem network pools global computing power and enables users to access these resources with GNT. Token holders pay resource owners to complete tasks requiring computational resources. The network is composed of the aggregated power of user devices. Golem is reportedly able to compute tasks that run the gamut from CGI rendering to machine learning. Transactions between participants are deemed to be safe because computations take place in sandbox environments that are sequestered from hosts' systems.